L.I.F.E.

(Live in Faith Everyday)

By:

Margie Carmichael Bailey

ISBN 978-0-557-58824-4

L.I.F.E.

(Live in Faith Everyday)

By:

Margie Carmichael Bailey

L. I.F.E.

(LIVE IN FAITH EVERYDAY)

The purpose and intent of this book is for you, the reader, to be able to use the acronyms and their meaning in your everyday life situations. My prayer is for this book to be used as a way, a means, as an instrument for uplifting you when the challenges and difficult times come into your life.

The words in this book are meant to inspire you and to encourage a new way of thinking about life, about God and about faith. The acronyms and their meanings are presented in an easy way that they can be remembered and used throughout the day. Sometimes during the course of your busy day you can use a quick jolt of inspiration. This book is designed to help you through your day and hopefully through your life's journey.

Take these thoughts and use them in your daily life. When fear, doubt, confusion enters your mind select an acronym and think about it These are words we are all familiar with and they can be used easily. My hope is that the words will find a place in your life and in your heart and give you strength and courage to face any of life's many challenges. My mother would often say, the more you spend with God the more time He will spend with you. Spend time with God today.

We can choose to live in faith or we can decide to live in fear. What is your choice today? Take time to write down your thoughts on faith and fear. Each page has a space for you to write down your thoughts. Use this opportunity to explore how you want to live.

This book is dedicated to my family, my husband Raymond, our sons Corey and Terrell, and our daughter- in law, Michele and our granddaughters, Nikori, Naishia and Shanaya. And to my dearly departed mother,

Constance Deborah Wilmatine Rebecca Thomas, who left this Earth in August 2003.

My prayer is for this book to be used as an instrument to help my family and you in your daily walk with God.

Enjoy and walk with God every day.

A.L.L.

Always Love Life

My thoughts are

B.A.L.L.

Blessings Always Lift Life

My thoughts are

C.A.L.L.

Christ Almighty, Loving Lord

My thoughts are

C.A.L.L.

Christ Always Lifts Life

My thoughts are

C.A.M.E.

Christ Answers Miracles Everyday

My thoughts are

C.A.P.E.

Christ Answers Prayers Everyday

My thoughts are

C.A.R.E.

Christ Always Responds Everyday

My thoughts are

C.O.M.E.

Christ Only Mends Errors

My thoughts are

C.A.P.E.

Christ Answers Prayer Everyday

My thoughts are

F.A.I.T.H.

Facing All Issues Through Him

My thoughts are

F.A.I.T.H.

Father Answers Instantly To Help

My thoughts are

F.A.L.L.

Father Always Loves Life

My thoughts are

F.A.L.L.

Faith Always Lift Life

My thoughts are

F.A.R.E.

Faith Always Responds Everyday

My thoughts are

F.E.A.R.

Father Empowers And Reunites

My thoughts are

F.E.A.R.

Father Encourages And Reunites

My thoughts are

F.E.A.R.

Father Encourages And Reassures

My thoughts are

F.E.E.D.

Faith Emerges Every Day

My thoughts are

F.E.E.D.

Faith Energizes Every Day

My thoughts are

F.L.O.W.E.R.

Find Love Openly With Every Role

My thoughts are

G.I.F.T.

God Is Faithful Today

My thoughts are

G.I.F.T.

God Is Forever Today

My thoughts are

G.I.V.E.

God Is Virtually Everywhere

My thoughts are

G.R.A.C.E.

God's Riches At Christ's Experience

My thoughts are

H.E.A.R.

Have Empathy And Respect

My thoughts are

H.E.R.E.

Heavenly Eternity Really Exists

My thoughts are

L.I.F.E.

Live In Faith Everyday

My thoughts are

L.I.F.E.

Let Inside Faith Emerge

My thoughts are

L.E.G.

Let Energy Go

My thoughts are

L.E.G.

Let Energy Grow

My thoughts are

L.I.L.L.Y.

Let Inside Living Lift You

My thoughts are

L.O.V.E.

Life Opens Vividly Everyday

My thoughts are

L.O.V.E.

Let Only Victory Emerge

My thoughts are

M.A.L.L.

Miracles Always Lift Life

My thoughts are

O.C.C.U.R.

Only Christ Can Utter Release

My thoughts are

P.R.A.Y.

Praise Really Answers You

My thoughts are

R.A.I.N.

Right Attitude Increases Naturally

My thoughts are

R.E.S.T.

Release Everyday Stress Today

My thoughts are

R.I.C.E.

Rest In Christ Everyday

My thoughts are

R.I.C.H.

Rest In Christ's Hands

My thoughts are

R.I.C.H.

Rest In Christ's Heart

My thoughts are

R.I.C.H.

Rest In Christ's Heaven

My thoughts are

R.I.D.E.

Relax In Divine Energy

My thoughts are

S.A.N.D.

Sing And Never Die

My thoughts are

S.A.N.D.

Smile And Never Die

My thoughts are

S.A.N.D.

Sing And Never Doubt

My thoughts are

S.A.N.D.

Smile And Never Doubt

My thoughts are

S.E.E.D.

Seek Eternal Energy Daily

My thoughts are

S.E.L.F.

Seeking Eternal Life Forever

My thoughts are

S.E.L.F.

Seeking Eternal Life Faithfully

My thoughts are

S.E.L.F.

Seeking Eternal Life Freely

My thoughts are

S.E.L.F.

Seeking Eternal Life Fearlessly

My thoughts are

S.E.L.F.

Seeking Eternal Love Freely

My thoughts are

S.E.L.F.

Seeking Eternal Love Forever

My thoughts are

S.E.L.F.

Seeking Eternal Love Faithfully

My thoughts are

S.L.E.E.P.

Silence Lets Everyone Enjoy Peace

My thoughts are

S.L.E.E.P.

Spiritual Love Engulfs Encourages People

My thoughts are

S.L.E.E.P.

Savior's Love Enlightens Everyone's Prayers

My thoughts are

S.M.A.R.T.

Spiritual Matters Are Really Timeless

My thoughts are

S.M.I.L.E.

Spiritual Matter Involves Living Everyday

My thoughts are

S.M.I.L.E.

Spiritual Mediation Is Living Everyday

My thoughts are

S.M.I.L.E.

Seek Miracles In Life Everyday

My thoughts are

T.I.M.E.

This I Must Experience

My thoughts are

T.I.M.E.

Try Inner Mediation Everyday

My thoughts are

W.A.T.E.R.

Wait And Treat Everyone Right

My thoughts are

W.A.T.E.R.

Worship And Treat Everyone Right

My thoughts are

W.H.E.N.

Worship Him Every Night

My thoughts are

I hope you have enjoyed the words in this book. It has been my deep desire to give you a way of touching the inner part of yourself and to draw upon your strength.

My prayers are with all who read this book entitled, L.I.F.E. (Live in Faith Everyday) that you grow spiritually and Live In Faith Everyday.

www.ingramcontent.com/pod-product-compliance
Ingram Content Group UK Ltd.
Pitfield, Milton Keynes, MK11 3LW, UK
UKHW041919190726
13854UKWH00003B/1340